Best Knock Knock Jokes for Kids

Good Clean Fun

Best Joke Book For Kids 2

Peter MacDonald

ISBN-13: 978-1492904458
ISBN-10: 1492904457

Other Books by Peter MacDonald

Best Joke Book for Kids : Best Funny Jokes and Knock Knock Jokes(200+ Jokes) Volume 1

Tongue Twisters For Kids ; Best Joke Book for Kids Volume 3

Introduction

Knock Jokes have been around for years, They say the first known knock knock jokes were recorded in 1936.

Knock Knock Jokes are a clever play on words, or sounds that words make. They appeal to us because of the obscure abd sometimes cryptic meanings.

Best of all they are just plain funny.

I hope you have a load of laughs as you read this book

Peter MacDonald

Knock Knock Jokes For Kids

Knock, knock.

Who's there?
Scold.
Scold who?
S'cold out here!

Knock, knock.

Who's there?
The dog.
The dog who

The dog doesn't go who, the dog goes woof!.

Knock, knock.

Who's there?

Boo.

Boo who?

Oh, don't get sad and cry, it's just a joke!

Knock, knock.

Who's there?

Interrupting sheep.

Interrupting she...

Baaaaaaaaaa!

Knock, knock.

Who's there?

Who.

Who Who?

Why are you acting like an owl if you are not one?

Knock, knock.

Who's there?

Where what.

Where what who?

You sound a bit confused.

Knock, knock.

Who's there?

Figs.

Figs who?

Figs the bell and I will no longer have to knock.

Knock, knock.

Who's there?

Abbott.

Abbott who?

Abbott the right time to answer your door.

Knock, knock.

Who's there?

Ada.

Ada who?

Ada burger for dinner.

Knock, knock.

Who's there?

Broccoli.

Broccoli who?

Since when does broccoli have a last name?

Knock, knock.

Who's there?

Olive.

Olive who?

Olive right across the street.

Knock, knock.

Who's there?

Interrupting pirate.

Interrupting pir…

Arrrrrrghhh!

Knock, knock.

Who's there?

Agatha.

Agatha who?

Agatha very bad headache. Do you have some pills?

Knock, knock.

Who's there?

Aida.

Aida who?

Aida lot of pizza and now my tummy hurts.

Knock, knock.

Who's there?

Al.

Al who?

Al give you a hug, just open that door, please!

Knock, knock.

Who's there?

Phillip.

Phillip who?

Phillip my bag with candy and chocolate!

Knock, knock.

Who's there?

Who who who.

Who who who who?

Why are you being so rude?

Knock, knock.

Who's there?

Lettuce.

Lettuce who?

Lettuce in, it's freezing out here!

Knock, knock.

Who's there?

Toaf.

Toaf who?

Tofu? What's wrong with eating meat?.

Knock, knock.

Who's there?

Cows.

Cows who?

Oh, no, cows don't who, cows go moo!.

Knock, knock.

Who's there?

Cash.

Cash who?

Oh thank, you, but I prefer walnuts!

Knock, knock.

Who's there?

Ken.

Ken who?

Ken I come in?.

Knock, knock.
Who's there?
Aldo.
Aldo who?
Aldo anything for you!

Knock, knock.
Who's there?
Merry.
Merry who?
Merry Christmas to all of you!

Knock, knock.
Who's there?
Needle.
Needle who?
Needle little food and a little money.

Knock, knock.
Who's there?
Roach.
Roach who?
I roach you a long letter, did you get it?

Knock, knock.
Who's there?
Etch.
Etch who?
Bless you!

Knock, knock.
Who's there?
Anee.
Anee who?
Anee one you like!

Knock, knock.
Who's there?
Nana.
Nana who?
It's nana your business.

Knock, knock.

Who's there?

Claire.

Claire who?

Claire the way, I am Coooming Thru!

Knock, knock.

Who's there?

Ya

Ya who?

Sure glad that you are so excited to see me!

Knock, knock.

Who's there?

Justin.

Justin who?

Justin the city and I came to visit you.

Knock, knock.

Who's there?

Alex.

Alex who?

Alex the questions here, this is not your job!

Knock, knock.
Who's there?
Ali.
Ali who?
Alligator!

Knock, knock.
Who's there?
Allied!
Allied who?
Allied, ok? Why don't you sue me?

Knock, knock.
Who's there?
Ashee.
Ashee who?
Oh, bless you!

Knock, knock.

Who's there?

Nobel.

Nobel who?

Nobel, that's why I am knocking on your door.

Knock, knock.

Who's there?

Lettuce.

Lettuce who?

Well, lettuce in and you will soon find out!

Knock, knock.

Who's there?

Anita.

Anita who?

Anita borrow a cup of sugar from you.

Knock, knock.

Who's there?

Annie.

Annie who?

Annie thing that you can do, I can do much better than you!

Knock, knock.
Who's there?
Cher.
Cher who?
Cher would be nice if you come out here!

Knock, knock.
Who's there?
Amarillo.
Amarillo who?
Amarillo nice girl/guy.

Knock, knock.
Who's there?
Althea.
Althea who?
Althea, if you are nice to me!

Knock, knock.

Who's there?

Alva.

Alva who?

Alva pear.

Knock, knock.

Who's there?

Amana.

Amana who?

Amana a really bad mood today!

Knock, knock.

Who's there?

Mickey.

Mickey who?

Mickey doesn't fit in the lock and this is why you have to open the door.

Knock, knock.

Who's there?

Ice cream.

Ice cream who?

Ice cream if you don't open the door.

Knock, knock.

Who's there?

Luke.

Luke who?

If you luke through the keyhole, you will see!

Knock, knock.

Who's there?

Amy.

Amy who?

Amy fraid of the dark. Please let me in!

Knock, knock.

Who's there?

Andrew.

Andrew who?

Andrew a picture of you!.

Knock, knock.

Who's there?

Kent.

Kent who?

Kent you tell by the sound of my voice?.

Knock, knock.

Who's there?

Isabel.

Isabel who?

Isabel working? I had to knock on the door first.

Knock, knock.

Who's there?

Carl.

Carl who?

Car'l get you there much faster than a bike would.

Knock, knock.

Who's there?

Tiss.

Tiss who?

Oh, do you have a cold?

Knock, knock.

Who's there?

Radio.

Radio who?

Radio not, here I come!

Knock, knock.

Who's there?

Annie.

Annie who?

Annie one just like you!

Knock, knock.

Who's there?

Arthur.

Arthur who?

Arthur any more people like you?

Knock, knock.

Who's there?

Dishes.

Dishes who?

Dishes the police, open the door!

Knock, knock.

Who's there?

Arbus.

Arbus who?

Arbus leaves in 10 minutes, hurry up!

Knock, knock.

Who's there?

Evvie.

Evvie who?

Evvie thing I do, I do for you!

Knock, knock.

Who's there?

Doughnut.

Doughnut who?

Doughnut ask me questions, come out and see for yourself!

Knock, knock.

Who's there?

Atlas.

Atlas who?

Atlas its Saturday!

Knock, knock.

Who's there?

Bean.

Bean who?

Bean to the market lately?

Knock, knock.

Who's there?

Bera

Bera who?

Bera necessities!

Knock, knock.

Who's there?

Shelby.

Shelby who?

Shelby coming around the mountain when she comes!

Knock, knock.

Who's there?

Dewey.

Dewey have to keep on telling these knock knock jokes?

Knock, knock.

Who's there?

I-8.

I-8 who?

I-8 breakfast already. Are we going to have lunch?

Knock, knock.
Who's there?
I love.
I love who?
Why who, I love you!

Knock, knock.
Who's there?
Norma Lee.
Normal Lee who?
Norma Lee I don't knock, I ring the bell.

Knock, knock.
Who's there?
Your mama.
Your mama who?
It's really your mama, baby, open the door!

Knock, knock.

Who's there?

Howie.

Howie who?

Howie going to get inside?

Knock, knock.

Who's there?

Hawaii.

Hawaii who?

I'm fine, thank you, Hawaii you?

Knock, knock.

Who's there?

Betty.

Betty who?

Betty you can't really tell who it is!

Knock, knock.

Who's there?

Ben.

Ben who?

Ben wondering what you are about to do.

Knock, knock.

Who's there?

Pecan.

Pecan who?

Hey, pecan somebody your own size!.

Knock, knock.

Who's there?

Repeat.

Repeat who?

Who, who!

Knock, knock.

Who's there?

Eileen.

Eileen who?

Eileen on the door and I break it!

.

Knock, knock

Who's there?

Cereal.

Cereal who?

Cereal, real nice pleasure to meet you!

Knock, knock.

Who's there?

Orange.

Orange who?

Orange you glad to see me?

Knock, knock.

Who's there?

Banana split.

Banana split who?

Banana split so ice creamed!

Knock, knock.

Who's there?

Theodore.

Theodore who?

Theodore's stuck and I can't open it!

Knock, knock.

Who's there?

Carrie.

Carrie who?

Carrie the garbage to the trash bean, please!

Knock, knock.

Who's there?

Cash.

Cash who?

Cash me if you can.

Knock, knock.

Who's there?

Tank.

Tank who?

You are more than welcome!

Knock, knock.

Who's there?

Harry.

Harry who?

Harry up and open the door!

Knock, knock.

Who's there?

Butter.

Butter who?

I butter not tell you or you'll get mad!

Knock, knock.

Who's there?

I scream.

I scream who?

I scream with chocolate sauce!

Knock, knock.
Who's there?
Lass
Lass who?
Oh, are you a cowboy?

Knock, knock.
Who's there?
Callum.
Callum who?
I'll Callum back.

Knock, knock.
Who's there?
Never.
Never who?
Never mind.

Knock, knock.

Who's there?

Icon.

Icon who?

Icon tell you but why don't you guess?.

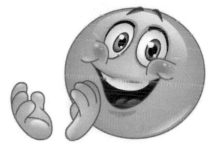

Knock, knock.

Who's there?

Despair.

Despair who?

Despair tiro just went flat and I can't drive home.

Knock, knock.

Who's there?

Ice cream.

Ice cream who?

Ice cream every time I see you.

Knock, knock.
Who's there?
Chile.
Chile who?
Chile out!

Knock, knock.
Who's there?
A little girl (boy).
A little girl (boy) who?
A little girl (boy) who can't reach the doorbell!

Knock, knock.
Who's there?
Chopin.
Chopin who?
Chopin in the supermarket.

Knock, knock.
Who's there?
Abbey.
Abbey who?
Abbey stung me on the arm!

Knock, knock.

Who's there?

Carlotta

Carlotta

Carlotta trouble every time it breaks down!

Knock, knock.

Who's there?

Jilly.

Jilly who?

It's really Jilly out here, let me in!

Knock, knock.

Who's there?

Ben.

Ben who?

Ben away for a long, long time!

Knock, knock.

Who's there?

Dozen.

Dozen who?

Dozen anyone want to let me in?

Knock, knock.

Who's there?

Adore.

Adore who?

Adore is between the two of us.

Knock, knock.

Who's there?

Two-knee.

Two-knee who?

A can of two-knee fish!

Knock, knock.

Who's there?

Honey bee.

Honey bee who?

Honey bee a dear and open the door for me!

Knock, knock
Who's there?
A heard.
A heard who?
A heard you were in town so I decided to come by!

Knock, knock.
Who's there?
Iva.
Iva who?
Iva runny nose from the cold out here, open the door!

Knock, knock.
Who's there?
Canoe.
Canoe who?
Canoe help me with the shopping?

Knock, knock.
Who's there?
Noah.
Noah who?
Noah good pizza place. Want to go for lunch?

Knock, knock.

Who's there?

Owls.

Owls who?

But of course owls who, what else would they do?

Knock, knock.

Who's there?

Chuck.

Chuck who?

Chuck the door, is it locked?

Knock, knock.

Who's there?

Water.

Water who?

Water you doing there, this is my house?

Knock, knock.

Who's there?

Sasha.

Sasha who?

Sasha fuzz! I just knocked on the door!

Knock, knock.

Who's there?

Ears.

Ears who?

Ears a lot more of those knock knock jokes for you!

Knock, knock.

Who's there?

Ralph.

Ralph who?

Ralph, Ralph, Ralph! I'm the dog!

Knock, knock.

Who's there?

B-4.

B-4 who?

Open the door B-4 I freeze!

Knock, knock.

Who's there?

Spell.

Spell who?

Oh, that's easy – W, H, and O!

Knock, knock.

Who's there?

Tennis who?

Tennis easy – five plus five!

Knock, knock.

Who's there?

Costa.

Costa who?

Costa lot to repair the doorbell!

Will you remember me in an hour?

Yes!

Will you remember me in a day?

Yes!

Will you remember me in a month?

Yes!

Knock, knock,

Who's there?

See, you already forgot me!

ABOUT THE AUTHOR

Peter MacDonald loves a good laugh, especially ones he can share with his children. He is committed to creating good clean fun in His series of joke books, "Best Joke Books For Kids". Peter is an Aussie with a good sense of Humor and he enjoys the good things in life, especially his church and family.